Mama's Portraits and Me
The Legacy, Life, and Love of Artist Carolyn Coffield Mends

By
Ekuwah Mends Moses

EduMatch®

Mama's Portraits and Me: The Legacy, Life, and Love of Artist Carolyn Coffield Mends
by Ekuwah Mends Moses
Published by EduMatch®
PO Box 150324, Alexandria, VA 22315

www.edumatch.org

ISBN: 978-1-953852-73-1

This book is dedicated to anyone who finds themself coping with grief and the loss of a loved one. May this be an example of a creative way to celebrate life.

1998
Carolyn Coffield Mends and
Ekuwah Mends Moses (bride)

Dear Reader,

Thank you for choosing to read a biography about a remarkable African-American woman. I loved my mother with my full heart although it did not always show to my family and friends.

At school, I was an honor student and received excellent behavior grades. At home, like many children, it was a different story. I yelled and refused to listen to my mother on a regular basis. I did not know how to express my feelings. I saw Mama's hands and legs progressively not cooperating with the desires of her brain and heart. It frustrated me. I chose to run and hide instead of helping her as much as I could. I wish I would have acted with more compassion and patience when I was a child. I am thankful she loved me and never held a grudge against me.

I write to cope with the sadness and regret in my adult heart. I write to comfort children and teens who are growing up with a loved one who has a chronic illness. I write for those who have lost a family member due to death or separation. I write for anyone who knows someone struggling with challenging feelings. I write to remind us to forgive ourselves, learn as we grow, and grant ourselves grace for what we didn't know. I write to honor my mother's life, express my gratitude, and inform my own children.

Navigating through Mama's old albums and home studio, to design the pages of this book, was emotionally stirring and bittersweet. My family and friends supported me during the design process, and I am grateful. I want this book to give people ideas for preserving family history and ways to cope with grief. May it inspire readers to persevere through obstacles. I aim for it to be an example of Black excellence and legacy.

All my best,

Ekuwah Mends Moses

CAROLYN COFFIELD MENDS
The Artist

I notice a girl who is Black like me.
What inspired Mama to paint her portrait?
Was it her unique green eyes?

Who is she?
What is her name?
What is she looking at?
Where is she going?
Is she quiet and shy like me?

So many questions flood my mind. I want to go back in time and ask Mama about this portrait and other pieces of her work. I will share what I do know about some of Mama's portraits.

SUSAN SILVERS/staff

LOCAL ARTIST CAROLYN Coffield (Mrs. Albion Mends), Warrensburg, will exhibit her artwork at the first regional Black Expo USA in Kansas City on Nov. 21 and 22. Her works include acrylic, watercolor and pastel portraits, mixed media and wood collages.

Courtesy of Warrensburg Star-Journal
Tuesday, November 17, 1992

"Green Eyes"

People

Mends Is Artist, Advisor, Modern Woman

By SAMI COWAN
Star-Journal Staff Writer

Bark appears on a tree and small branches grow in several directions on the illustration board as Carolyn Mends leans over a half-finished watercolor landscape. "Art is my passion," she admits, "even though it is secondary to my employment."

One of the people she would most like to talk to would be the artist Rembrandt she says. "I like his use of light and color."

Black history books spill over the floor as she leafs through a magazine looking for an article about a woman she would like to know. Mary McLeod Behune's picture comes out from under her fingers as she explains why this woman started a college in Florida and led a full life on...

Leading a new idea to Mends is not a new idea. As a teacher of art, she not only advises students in out their classes at Central Missouri State University, but serves as a role model and mentor for those who come from families who have not had much exposure, blacks, she says. For those students only known what they see on television or in the newspapers. "I want them to have an open mind and be willing to experience different things," she says.

Mends fills many roles. She spends her days advising students at CMSU, her evenings recording landscapes and people on canvas at home, supporting her husband...

age for her two daughters.

Carolyn Coffield Mends was born in Hobbs, N.M., Jan. 3, 1951, one of four girls. She graduated from eastern New Mexico University in 1972 with a commercial art degree and received her masters in art education in 1974. Albion Mends Jr. was in a class she taught...

York with a Jamaican minister in his family. And she planned to be a commercial artist. Instead, she and her husband, moved to Warrensburg and found a job as an advisor at CMSU in 1974.

"Getting married was a changing experience," she said. "...'I do,' you..."

The artist known as Carolyn Coffield was my mama. She also signed professional artwork with her initials - CAC. The 1960s through the 1990s were the peak of her artistic career.

According to Aunt Jan, Mama used crayons to create this self-portrait while she was in college.

Easter Vacation to see Grandmama and Aunt Jan

April 13-15, 1979

When I was young, our family took several summer road trips from Missouri to New Mexico. These trips were one of the ways I learned more about Mama's life before my birth.

During these trips, I explored Mama's family history, art education, cultural environment, and the Southwest.

Mama met her father for the first time in 1992

SUMMER 1992

Back home to New Mexico — here in Portales, ENMU

EASTERN NEW MEXICO UNIVERSITY
Carolyn A. Coffield
Hobbs

1972
Summa cum laude graduate

COLORADO

KANSAS

MISSOURI

NEW MEXICO

OKLAHOMA

Hobbs NM

TEXAS

after a DECADE
JULY 2 - 15, 1992

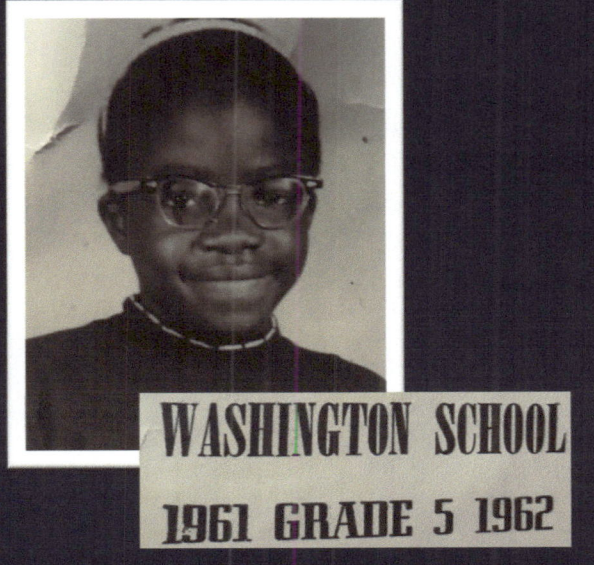

WASHINGTON SCHOOL
1961 GRADE 5 1962

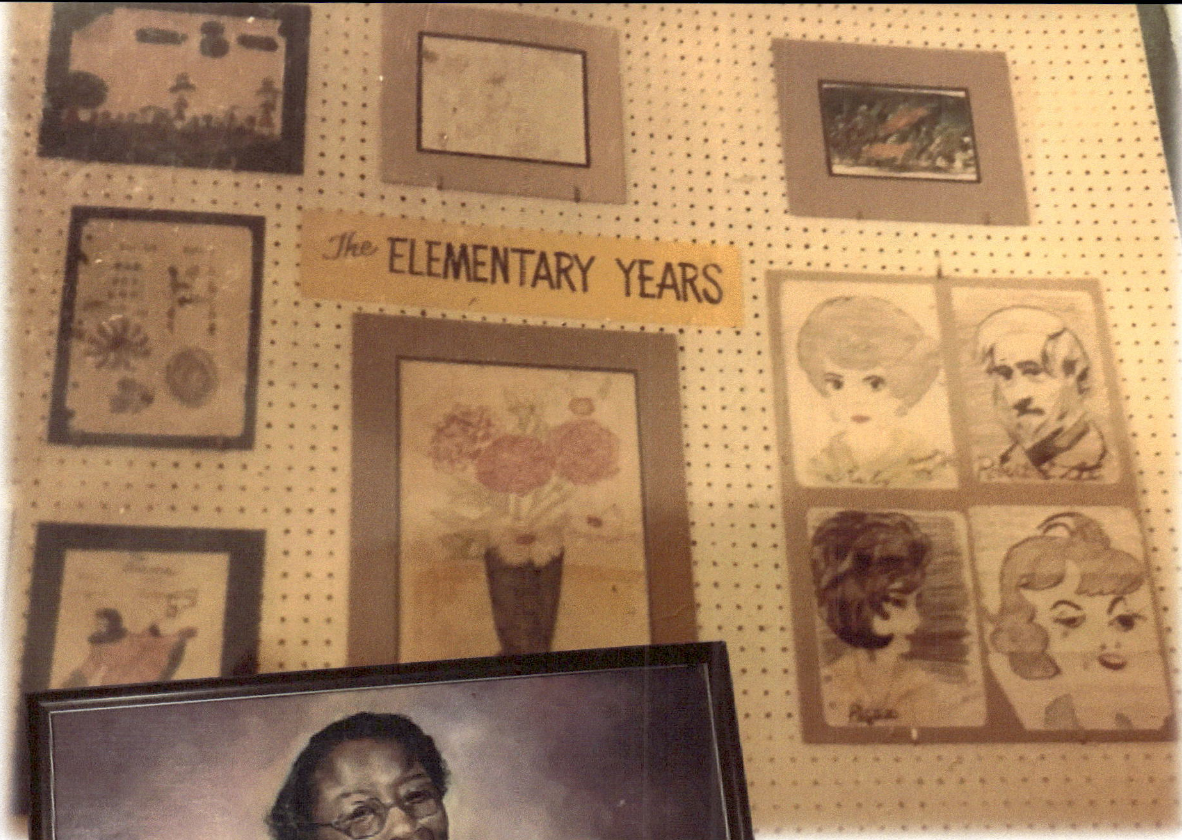
The ELEMENTARY YEARS

Mama always told me about how Grandma encouraged her to do well in school and follow her dreams. These are values Mama passed on to me as well. Art was an important part of Mama's life from an early age.

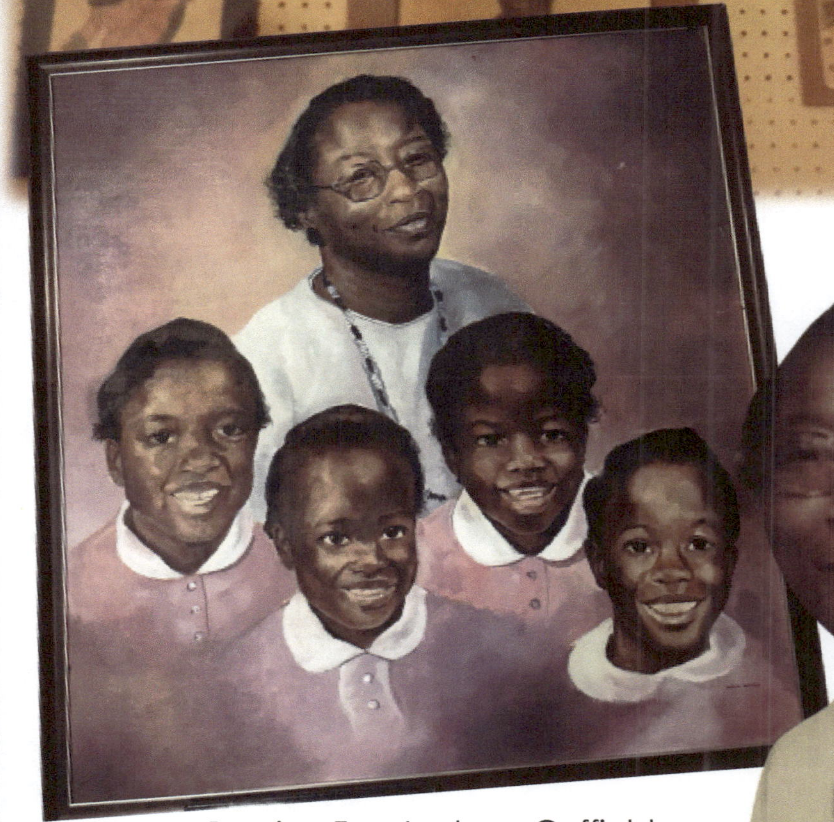

Bernice Fay Jackson Coffield
(my grandmother and her four girls)

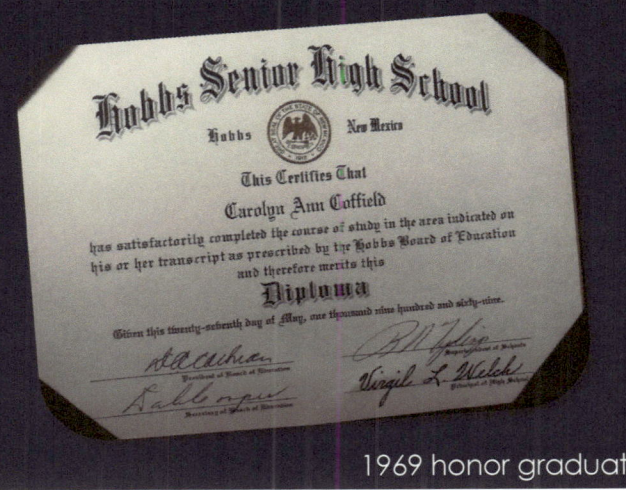

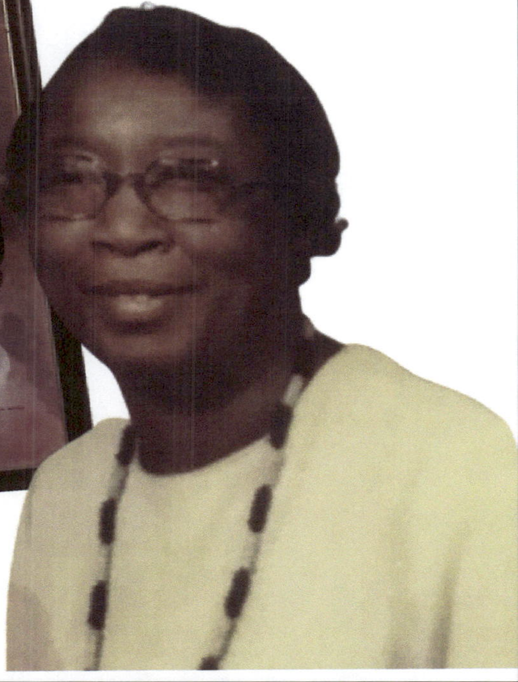

Hobbs Senior High School

Hobbs New Mexico

This Certifies That

Carolyn Ann Coffield

has satisfactorily completed the course of study in the area indicated on his or her transcript as prescribed by the Hobbs Board of Education and therefore merits this

Diploma

Given this twenty-seventh day of May, one thousand nine hundred and sixty-nine.

President of Board of Education — Superintendent of Schools

Secretary of Board of Education — Virgil L. Welch, Principal of High School

1969 honor graduate

My grandmother, Bernice Fay Jackson Coffield, raised four girls as a single parent in Hobbs, New Mexico. I remember my grandma's high expectations and running errands with her during the summer vacations.

Writing letters
With Grandma at work

Summer 1985

Hi MOM HOW ARE YOU? WE ARE O.K I LOVE YOU. HOW ARE WE ARE OK WE LOVE YOU WITH WE MISS YOU WE ARE GREAT WORK WITH GRANDMOTHER LOVE KuWalh

Walking down Grandma's dark hallway, I got shivers while looking into the eyes of Ms. Rutelia Nunley. The combination of the hallway's darkness and her piercing eyes stopped me in my tracks. The painting made the hallway scary and feel like someone was watching me.

I never met Auntie Jan's cousin, but I heard this kind and beautiful woman meant a lot to the entire family. Therefore, Mama painted Cousin Rutelia early in her life. Perhaps Grandma put this portrait at the end of the hallway to capture the essence of our elders.

CAROLYN COFFIELD

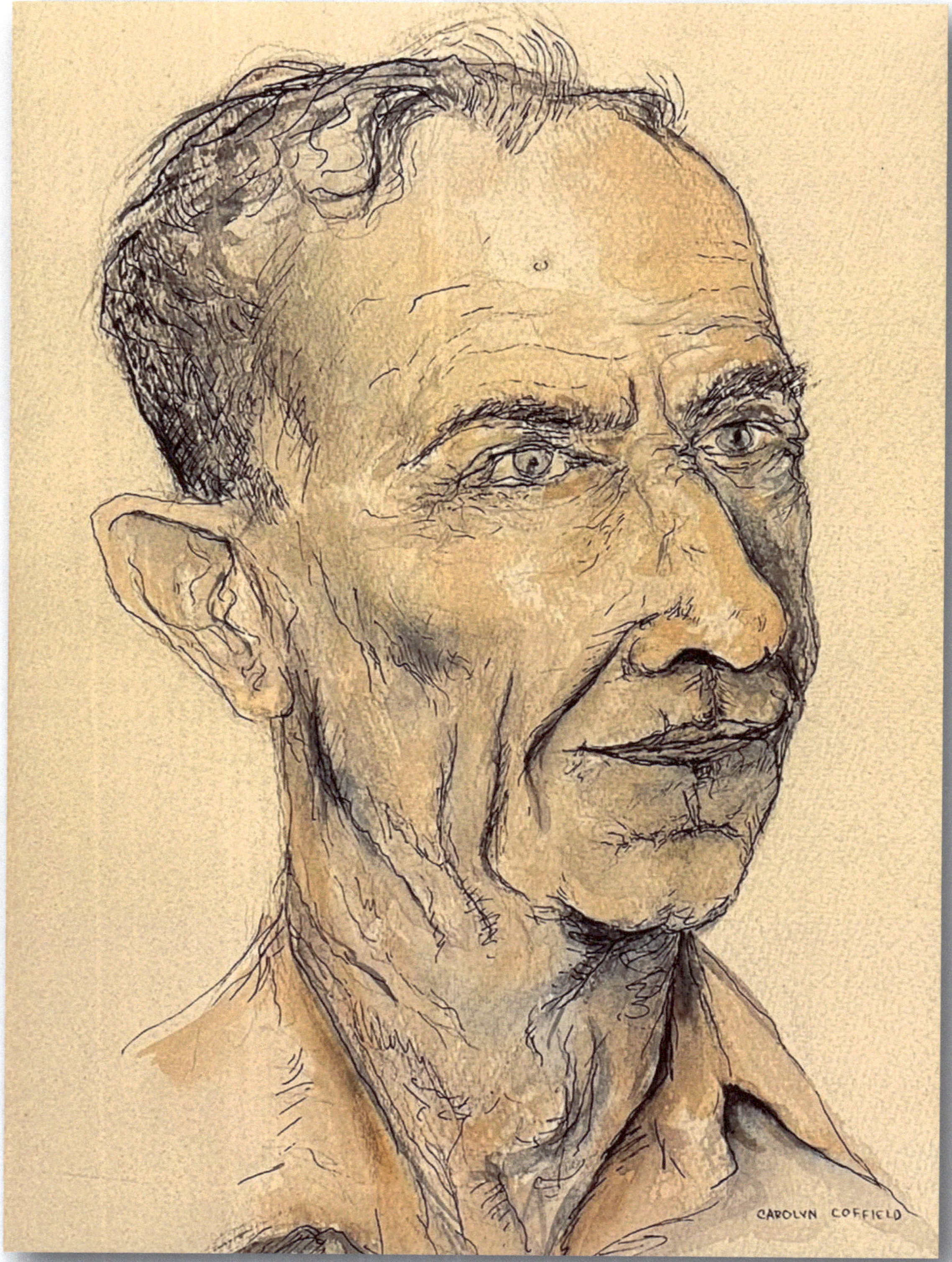

Mama's high school portfolio is impressive. As an honor student, her attention to detail made her work look realistic. She noticed the age lines, dimples, hairlines, scars, and the range of skin colors in her subjects. Mama also observed the leaves on trees, shadows, and the coldness of winter.

Hobbs High School
Art Show

CAROLYN COFFIELD

After high school, Mama was offered a scholarship to attend Eastern New Mexico University. She sold portraits to help pay for her tuition and expenses. Mama earned a degree in Commercial Art. She also earned an advanced degree in Art Education.

Romulo Guerra Villegas II

Rómulo

Gabriel

Irene

While Mama was in college, a man named Mr. Romulo Villegas II purchased several pieces of her artwork. Mr. Villegas asked his children to find Mama's family as a final wish before he passed away. In December 2021, I met his son, Romulo Villegas III, after his wife found me by searching on the internet. Romulo said "Purity" was a treasured painting that hung over his father's bed since the early 1970s.

Romulo II and Carolyn
1973

"Purity"

Romulo III and Ekuwah
2021

Mama's collegiate portfolio is a pictorial record of the 1960s and 1970s. She captured everything from Afros to bell-bottom pants to the Civil Rights Movement.

"LINK" – "CLARENCE WILLIAMS III"
Tempera Rendering

Bride and Groom

Mama met her future husband, my dad, while calling out the attendance roster at ENMU. He was a Ghanaian sprinter on the University's track team and enrolled in her graduate class. She captured Dad's likeness in several portraits over the years.

Albion Mends III

CAROLYN COPFIELD

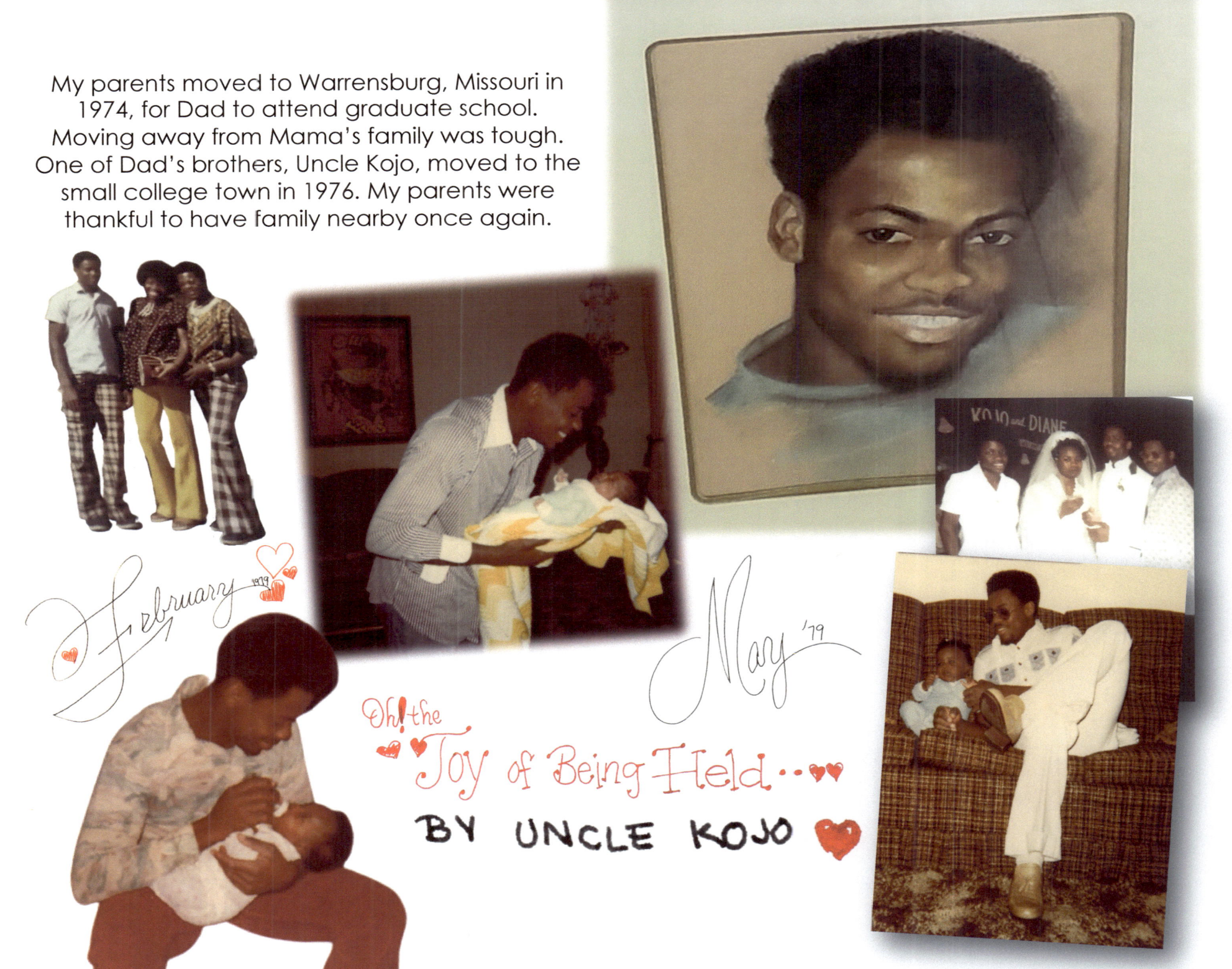

My parents moved to Warrensburg, Missouri in 1974, for Dad to attend graduate school. Moving away from Mama's family was tough. One of Dad's brothers, Uncle Kojo, moved to the small college town in 1976. My parents were thankful to have family nearby once again.

February 1979

May '79

Oh! the Joy of Being Held...

BY UNCLE KOJO

CAMDENTON--Ten area residents participated in an all-day art workshop Saturday on pastel portrait painting given by Carolyn Coffield Mends of Warrensburg. The event was sponsored by the Ozark Brush and Palette Club.

The Artist

CAROLYN COFFIELD

Mrs. Albion Mends

"Art is not for a select few. Art should be experienced, loved, and owned by all segments of society."
- Carolyn Coffield

ARTIST IN RESIDENCE—Mrs. Carolyn Coffield, artist in residence at the CMSU Union, has brought a new service to the University campus. She can usually be found working in the lobby from 8 a.m. to noon.

Artist In Residence Is On Duty In The Union

June 14, 1974

Nutrition Poster

Carbon copy

Artist Carl Munsen, Warrensburg, holds a pastel portrait of himself sketched in 45 minutes by Carolyn Coffield Mends, also of Warrensburg. The two were displaying their works at an art fair Saturday at the State Fair Shopping Center.

BLACK HISTORY: *A Blueprint for Survival*

Event Program Cover

Mama did a lot of graphic design work because covers, flyers, memes, and posters could not be created using online design programs like today. She also did speed drawing. This is when a portrait is completed in anywhere from thirty minutes to one hour using a live model or a photograph.

the Black VOICE

ISSUE NO. 4
CMSU - FEB. 1988

Inspired by the Black National Anthem "Lift Every Voice"

Verbal Opportunity of ABC to Inform and Congratulate through Encouragement

BLACK HISTORY MONTH

"FATHER OF BLACK HISTORY", CARTER GODWIN WOODSON was born of a poor family in Virginia. He wrote and studied at home and abroad. At the age of thirty-seven , Woodson earned a Ph.D from Harvard. In 1915, he founded the Association for the Study of Negro Life and History. In order to popularize the study of Black History, in 1926 he inaugurated Black History Week. By spreading knowledge of the widely-neglected history of American Blacks, he sought to foster respect for the ethnic backgrounds of all U.S. citizens. Honoring the ACHIEVEMENTS OF BLACK AMERICANS.

Feb.

1 YOLANDA KING Lecture, "A Dream Deferred", 7:30 PM, Hendricks Hall. ABC reception following in Union Faculty Lounge.

2 HARVI GRIFFIN, pop harpist and singer, 8 PM, Hart Recital Hall

3 ABC Gospel Choir BAKE SALE, Administration Building, 8-3

5 DR. GEORGE McKENNA Lecture, "Public Education Today, 8 PM, Science Aud. Principal, George Washington Prep. High School in Los Angeles.

8-12 DRUG AWARENESS WEEK

12-13 "BEVERLY HILLS COP I AND II"

19-20 "LILLIES OF THE FIELD"

24 ABC GOSPEL CHOIR BAKE SALE, Administration Building

26-27 "RUNNING SCARED"

28 ASHFORD AND SIMPSON present, "Reflections on Songwriting" 8 PM, Hall, Husband Wife

THE BLACK FLAG was created in 1921 by Marcus Garvey, born in Jamaica then came to New York. The colors:
BLACK - pride in the Black skin
RED - blood of Black race shed
GREEN - promise of a new, better life

BLACK NATIONAL ANTHEM -
"LIFT EV'RY VOICE" composed in 1900 by James Weldon and John Rosamond Johnson.

All are encouraged to participate in the events scheduled for Black History Month.

More, much more is being planned. GET IN-VOLVED WITH ABC and share your ideas! YOU ARE SOMEBODY! YOU ARE IMPORTANT!!

WELCOME TO CMSU ALL NEW STUDENTS FOR SPRING! ABC wishes you every success in your studies!

Newsletter

Marcus Mosiah Garvey
(1887-1940)

She used ink, pastels, acrylics, and watercolors to create incredible artwork. Mama also relied on a typewriter to complete some of her projects.

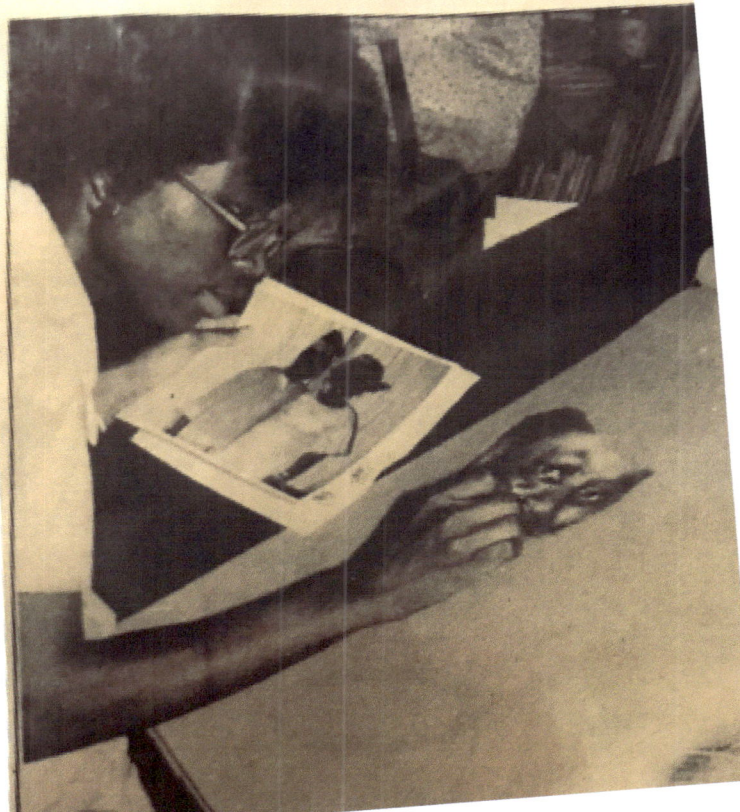

Mama liked all forms of art. Pastel portraiture was her specialty. She brought black and white photographs to life through various artistic mediums.

Courtesy of Warrensburg Star-Journal

Black History Month
Greeting Card

An Evening with
Maya
Angelou
NOVEMBER 21, 1991
7PM ~ HENDRICKS HALL

Event Banner

"Art is not a luxury. The artist is so necessary in our lives. The artist explains to us, or at least asks the questions which must be asked."
– Maya Angelou

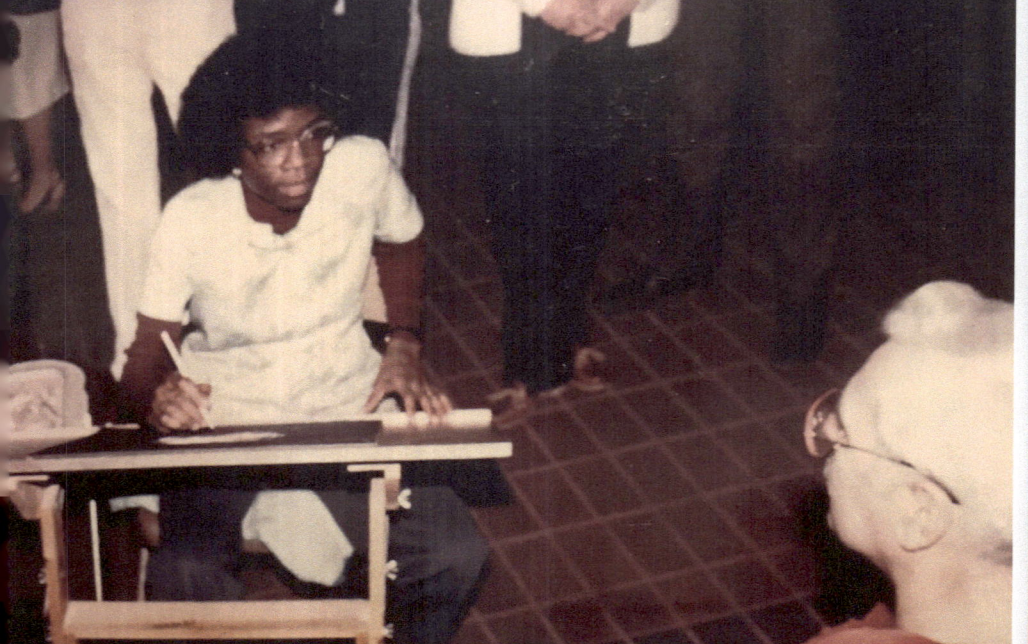

Sitting Pretty

Carolyn Mends, 208 Center Dr., demonstrated her artistic skill Saturday at the Johnson County Fall Festival. Here she paints a pastel portrait of Clarence Shirley, Kansas City. She is a member of Mid-Missouri Artists.

Mama knew it was difficult for subjects to sit still. She preferred to use models even though working from a photograph allowed her more time to complete the portrait.

"Photographs are limiting. You're dealing with some segment of time from the past. You must take into consideration the changes that have taken place."
- Carolyn Coffield

Mama's deep love for her family and friends was inspiring. She often painted portraits for birthday gifts and special occasions.

For Dada's 70th Birthday 1988

Gifts for my grandfather,
Albion Mends II
(portraits of my late grandmother)

Georgina Isabella Sagoe
(fondly known as "Auntie Nana Effuah")

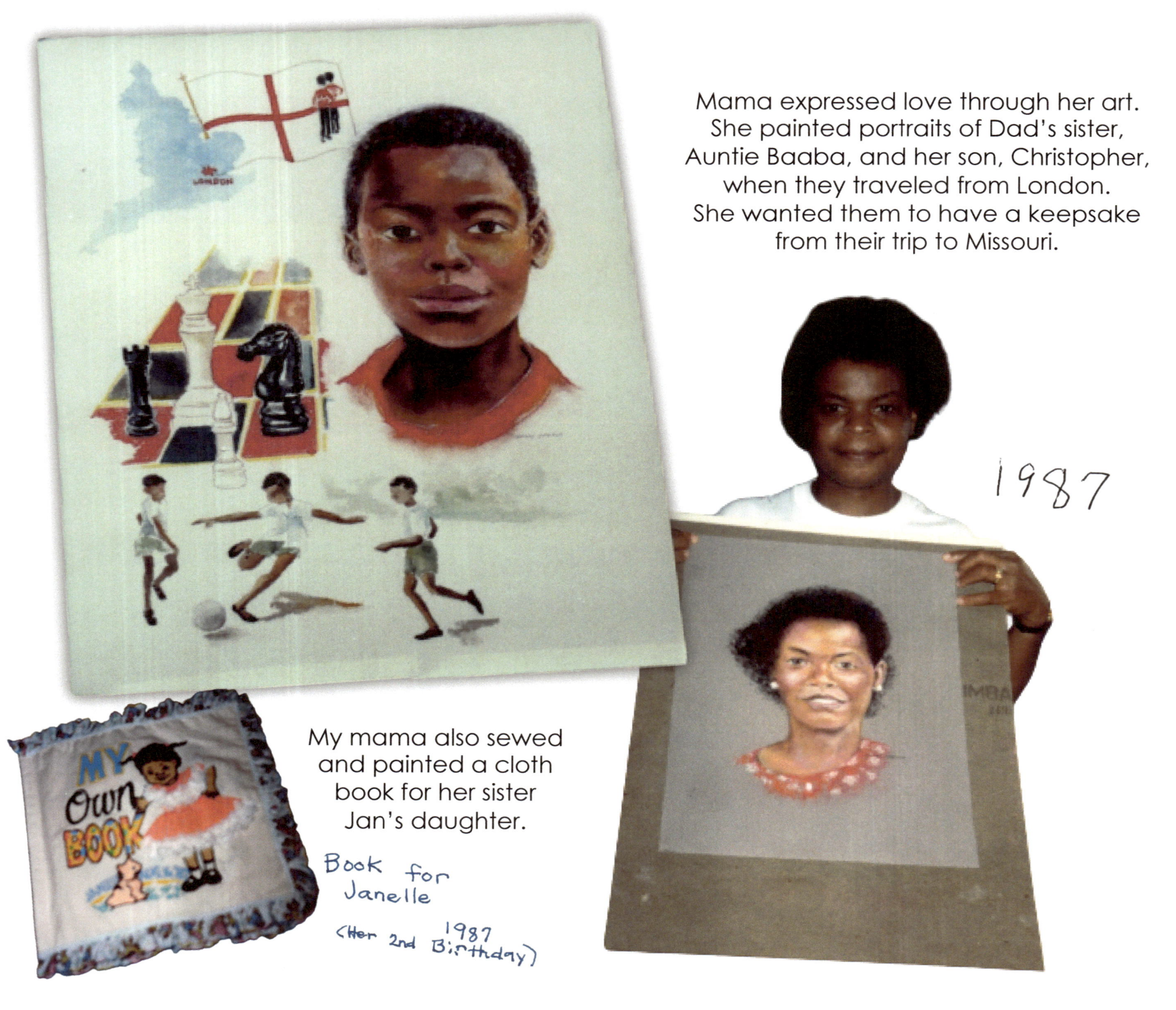

Mama expressed love through her art.
She painted portraits of Dad's sister,
Auntie Baaba, and her son, Christopher,
when they traveled from London.
She wanted them to have a keepsake
from their trip to Missouri.

1987

My mama also sewed
and painted a cloth
book for her sister
Jan's daughter.

Book for
Janelle
(Her 2nd Birthday) 1987

Art was Mama's true passion. I grew up watching my mama painting at her easel through the late-night hours; Mama's portraits and me.

JOJO'S PORTRAIT

That's me crawling on the shaggy carpet in the basement. Mama drew a pastel portrait of my father's cousin, Uncle Jojo, who was visiting from Virginia.

Dr. Ebenezer "Jojo" Asafu-Adjaye

AΦA crest and
FOUNDERS

July 1908

Mama invited people to our home to model or pick up commissioned work.

Mama also delivered
her framed artwork to
customers' homes.

"Carolyn Mends originals —
the center piece was done
while she was very young,
maybe early twenties, while the
outside two were added many
years later. We have been very
blessed to share her incredible
talent with friends and family."
- Carole E. Nimmer

1993

Newspapers, magazines, photographs, and other print media were sources of inspiration for Mama. She kept many filing cabinets and folders of her favorite images to reproduce. A Black woman and baby caught her eye in a 1968 black and white newspaper. In 1987, Mama entitled this award-winning painting "Love."

FIRST

WARRENSBURG
SPRING
ART
FESTIVAL

FINE
ARTS

BEST
OF
DISPLAY

1987

My mama was a persistent and courageous woman. She was strong like the women she admired, applauded, and amplified through her work.

Black History Program (cover)
February 21, 1988

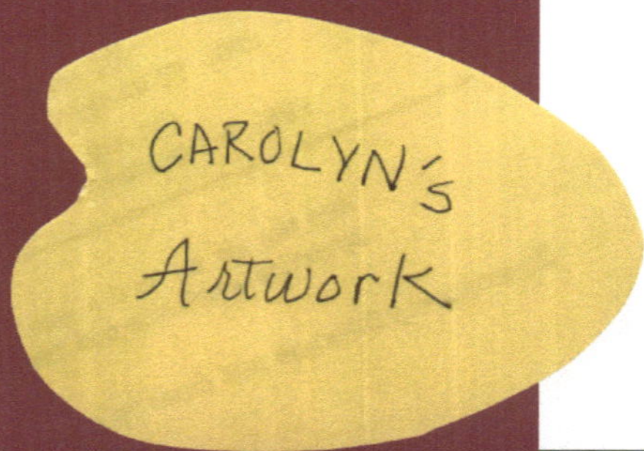

Mama's art paid tribute to her Black heritage.
Mary McLeod Bethune was one of the Black women
she read about in her vast collection of books.
She admired how Bethune dreamed of starting a
college and worked to make it happen. Mama had
dreams of serving others in different ways.

Mama won awards for her portraits. The pieces share the stories of courageous women from around the world. Looking back, I now realize how remarkable my mother was. She kept a relentless pace of production despite her advancing physical limitations.

The Knob Noster item

VOL. 41, NO. 34

KN Fair Winners
1998

Congratulations to the winners at the Art Show in Knob Noster, September 3rd, 4th and 5th

Carolyn Mends   Blue in Oil
Blue and White in Mixed Media
Red in Acrylic

"Because of Love"

It is possible that you have never heard of my mama or seen her artwork. Social media and search engines had not yet been invented during her most productive years. So, Mama could not sell or showcase her artwork online. She did the best she could to spread her love of people. Mama joined an art organization, gave lessons, participated in community events, and founded university organizations.

"STRENGTH OF AGE and WISDOM" (pastel)

ART FRIENDS

Mama believed that she was born with a natural artistic gift. The years of education and the people Mama met along the way nurtured the talent she was born with. She passionately shared her gift with others through teaching and service.

CAROLYN COFFELD

Mends' Art Focuses On African Heritage

Acrylics, watercolor and pastels are the media in which Carolyn Coffield Mends works. Her Warrensburg home serves as her studio.

One of her latest creative approaches is African fabric folk art, compositions that enhance the African heritage and lifestyle. (See above.)

Mends was born in Hobbs, N.M. in 1951. She earned her bachelor's and master's degrees in art education from Eastern New Mexico University in Portales, N.M.

She worked as an academic adviser at CMSU for 22 years, retiring on disability leave in 1996. She has been diagnosed with multiple sclerosis and now uses an electric scooter to give her more mobility.

She is a member of the local Mid-Missouri Art Association and exhibits, teaches and does work on commission.

PROFESSIONAL ARTIST OFFERING art lessons in my home studio. Call 660-

October 6, 1998
Courtesy of Warrensburg Star-Journal

In 1984, Mama opened her home studio to adults who wanted art lessons. She also facilitated pastel portrait workshops and demonstrations throughout Missouri.

CAROLYN'S ART STUDENTS 1984

Camdenton Junior High art classes

Mama encouraged families with young children to explore and create a variety of art forms.

Ekuwah's Self-Portrait
6/8/83

2001

As I grew, Mama gave me suggestions and assisted me with my school assignments. She helped me make posters, banners, and even enter an art contest. I always compared my ability to hers. I did not feel confident in my drawing abilities, but I realized that I am better at making crafts and design work. I have an eye for color, and I am talented in my own way.

Mama always wanted her art to reach as many people as possible. She looked for opportunities inside and outside of our hometown. I remember the task of safely stacking her work into our family's station wagon and trying to avoid scratching the custom framing.

"Peace Makers"

"Green Eyes"

Looking at first choice votes only:
Rank 1   Green Eyes by Carolyn Mends
Rank 2   Evening Primrose by Bobbie Baxter
Rank 3   Watermellon Respite by Carolyn Mends

    Several artists received votes for two or more paintings. The following artists received the highest cumulative scores:

    Rank 1   Carolyn Mends

Mid-Missouri Artists, Inc.
July 1990 Newsletter

"Watermelon Respite"

**Carolyn Mends
Guest Artist
at
Baxter Art Gallery
in
Butler, Missouri
through
April 30.**

April 1993

Mends Top Local Artist

Warrensburg artist Carolyn Mends was first-place winner in the professional division of the Third Annual Painting and Drawing Exhibition sponsored by Mid-Missouri Artists, Inc. The event was held on Saturday at the Margaret Long Arts and Crafts Center.

Courtesy of Warrensburg Star-Journal

FIRST PLACE

❖

MID-MISSOURI ARTIST INC.

19th Annual Christmas Arts & Crafts Sale

Sponsored by

Mid-Missouri Artists, Inc.

Saturday, November 12, 1994
9:00 a.m. to 5:00 p.m.

LOCATION:
CMSU Multi-Purpose Building
King and Washington Streets
Warrensburg, Missouri

Mama was an active member of the Mid-Missouri Artists, Inc. She participated in the events and community galleries. Mama enjoyed drawing at her easel during the annual shows. University students, faculty, alumni, and community members gathered around her each year. Mama's photo albums are full of the local newspaper's coverage of her participation and awards.

Professor Edward Daryl Duff is one of my mama's favorite past students. This is a photo of him visiting her booth at the Arts and Crafts Sale. Mama followed his achievements in the U.S. Navy Band Sea Chanters long after his 1989 college graduation.

Mama met many famous people during her life. Authors, athletes, astronauts, singers, politicians, comedians, and beauty queens visited our small town. She considered it a joy to honor their life's work through her art.

23 November 1994

Dear Mrs. Mends,

I hope this letter finds you doing well. My friend, Gina, just delivered the painting of Thurgood Marshall to me. Thank you for doing such a wonderful and thoughtful job on the painting. I love that your paintings always tell a story, and this one is a wonderful depiction of Thurgood's life.

Thurgood Marshall is a reminder to me; one that I can now see daily. One person can make a difference and each of us has a responsibility to do so.

Thank you again for the time, effort, and love that I know goes into each piece of work.

Sincerely,
Autumn

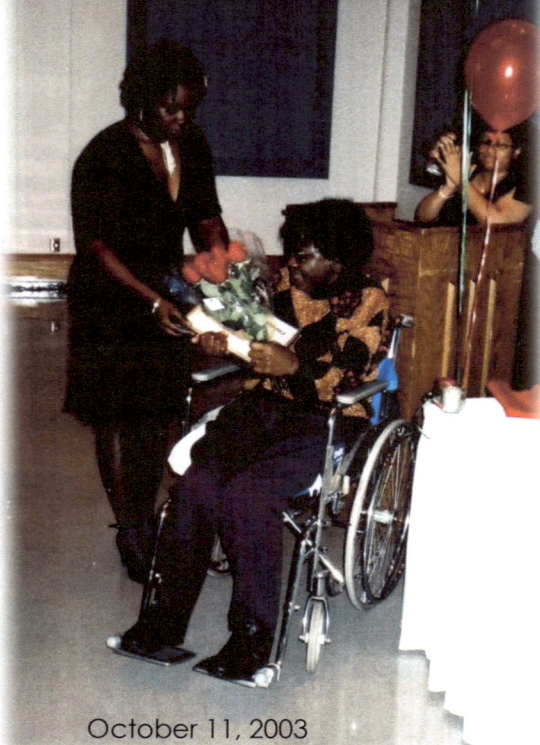

October 11, 2003

In 1975, doctors diagnosed Mama with Multiple Sclerosis (MS). Sharing her story is important to me because many people met her after the nerve damage kept her from producing fine art. Dad was her extraordinary primary caregiver for over seventeen years. I made sure Mama was surrounded by the artwork and family photos while he kept her comfortable.

Winter 2006

Upcoming Programs	pages 4-7
Keeping Stress in Check	page 7
Scholarship Winners	pages 8-9
Awareness Week	page 9
Medicare Update	page 10
Pregnancy & MS	page 11
Outstanding Volunteers	page 12
Missouri Tax Info	page 13
Year-End Giving	page 13
Get Involved!	page 15

NATIONAL MULTIPLE SCLEROSIS SOCIETY

msconnection
Mid America Chapter

Mid America Chapter Annual Meeting and Awards

Albion Mends of Warrensburg, Missouri was named **Carepartner of the Year** for providing outstanding care to his wife, Carolyn. Albion has been at Carolyn's side since her MS diagnosis in 1975. A professor at Central Missouri State University, he maintains involvement in community activities. In 2005, he and Carolyn were awarded the Dr. Martin Luther King Humanitarian Award from CMSU. "Without an understanding caregiver like my spouse, I may have been divorced or in a nursing home," says Carolyn. "But thank God, Albion is still here with me. I wish I could do more for him."

Albion Mends receives his award from Tami Greenberg and Senator Yvonne Wilson

National Multiple Sclerosis Society
www.nationalmssociety.org

Mama's MS did not define her. Instead, her positive attitude, unwavering resilience, remarkable courage, faithful service, and strength through adversity are part of her enduring legacy.

I am thankful for every remembrance of you.
Our paths have crossed as you passed my way.
The joy, smiles, and service that binds our lives and hearts together have been memorable and precious.

Different stages have been occurring in my life and I have been surrounded by angels and covered with prayer by well wishers and friends.

Be assured of my inner peace and a faith that has been strengthened.
Central is the center of hope for present and future generations.
Keep the vision and serve well.

Sincerely,

Mrs. Carolyn Mends

Mrs. Carolyn Mends

Farewell Reception
September 19, 1996

My dad's brother, Uncle Osa, was one of the most powerful speakers during Mama's funeral on July 22, 2017. He brought items on the stage and used them to celebrate her legacy. What touched my heart the most was the portrait she made of him in the 1970s.

May Moments with Family

2017

Our First Christmas – 1973 1009 S. Ave A., Portale, N.M.

1979

Memorial Weekend with Uncle Osa

(Clarence Mends)

Mama's paintings and portraits tell a timeless story, and I am on a quest to share her art in a way that she was never able to achieve. As the youngest of her two children, I am honored to call this gifted artist Mama.

December 2014
Ekuwah Mends Moses
Carolyn Coffield Mends

Through the years, I found my voice and gained confidence by watching Mama in action. You can see me in the photograph sucking my thumb when I was a little girl. My thumb and my blankie comforted me when I felt nervous, sad, scared, or sleepy.

"Oh Freedom"

I can relate to this angelic girl Mama drew.

Mama never complained about being nervous or scared of crowds of people. She always held her head high and seemed so confident. I felt like I was in the spotlight as strangers watched Mama speak. I was uncomfortable with people watching her draw. I have grown to admire Mama's strength and reflect on all that she modeled.

I'm in the spotlight!

Incomplete Painting:
South Africans on a historic
journey to the first-time vote.

Over the years, after reading through Mama's handwritten notes and looking through piles of incomplete paintings, here are the things I have learned:

1. **Inspiration can strike at any time. Creativity comes in bursts.**

2. **We all make mistakes, and they are valuable learning opportunities.**

3. **Have an open mind and be willing to experience challenges.**

4. **Be patient and always give your best.**

5. **Celebrate the success of yourself and others.**

Mama's Portraits and Me

Mama painted people who inspired her.
Mama painted people to express love and gratitude.
Mama painted people to preserve their stories.
Mama painted people until her hands lost grip.
Mama painted people so you and I would acknowledge and appreciate the beauty in the world.

Mama painted so we would learn to love our authentic selves.
Mama painted so we would learn how to give and receive love.
Mama painted so we would dare to dream.

CAROLYN COFFIELD MENDS views one of her paintings "They Dare to Dream," which is exhibited in the Ward Edwards Library on the Central Missouri State University campus. She says the painting was meant to depict the feeling that dreams can be fulfilled through children.

Wednesday, June 12, 1985
Courtesy of Warrensburg Star-Journal

"They Dare to Dream"
I am featured in the painting.

July 1983

Thank You

Mama's Portraits and Me was designed through a compilation of the professional art of the late Carolyn Coffield Mends **(CAC)**.

Contributors:
Albion Mends III
Effuah Sam
Warrensburg Star-Journal
Jan Austin
Carole E. Nimmer
Romulo Villegas III
Kojo and Diane Mends
Ama Elizabeth Mends
Grace Asafu-Adjaye

Ekuwah Mends Moses is the youngest daughter of Albion Mends III and the late Carolyn Coffield Mends (January 3, 1951 – July 13, 2017). She currently teaches and writes in Las Vegas, Nevada. Ekuwah enjoys traveling and spending quality time with her family. This is her second nonfiction picture book of her family's history. Contact her for inquiries about Carolyn's artwork. Follow her for more family stories and authentic compilations. Visit the website for a free teaching guide and related academic standards.

ekuwah.com

@Ekuwah

@ekuwah_m

Ekuwah Mends Moses, Author

#MamasPortraits

_____ Also available _____

My Name is an Address
By Ekuwah Mends Moses

www.ingramcontent.com/pod-product-compliance
Lightning Source LLC
Chambersburg PA
CBHW040817120626

46551CB00004B/585